COMING UP...

As you start a new year at school,
you are probably wondering what it will be like.
Use this page to write some of your thoughts
about the year to come.

Some things I hope will be the same as last year: _____

_____

_____

_____

Some things I expect to be different: _____

_____

_____

_____

Some things I hope to achieve this year: _____

_____

_____

_____

Some special plans I have: _____

_____

_____

_____

At the end of the year, I hope I can look back and say: _____

_____

_____

_____

1

Dr. Silverfish and his book are rather unusual. But they both attract Milo's attention. Use the information in the story to illustrate the back and front cover of Dr. Silverfish's book.

Dr. Silverfish does not look perfect to Milo. What do you think a perfect person would be like?

A perfect person would always _____

_____

A perfect person would never _____

_____

A perfect student would always _____

_____

A perfect student would never _____

_____

A perfect parent would always _____

_____

A perfect parent would never _____

_____

A perfect teacher would always _____

_____

A perfect teacher would never _____

_____

A perfect friend would always _____

_____

A perfect friend would never _____

_____

Other signs of perfection are:

_____

_____

_____

_____

_____

_____

_____

_____

_____

_____

_____

_____

_____

_____

_____

_____

_____

_____

YOU REALLY SHOULDN'T HAVE

What do you think Stewie, Alice, Billy, and Polly *really* thought about their presents? What might they have written if they had been honest? Write the thank-you letter each of them might have written, but never mailed!

Dear Grandmother,

_____

_____

_____

_____

_____

_____

_____

_____

_____

Love,
Stewie

Dear Uncle Barney,

_____

_____

_____

_____

_____

_____

_____

_____

_____

Yours truly,
Alice

Dear Mrs. Blorney,

_____

_____

_____

_____

_____

_____

_____

_____

                                    Sincerely,
                                    Billy

Dear Grandmother,

_____

_____

_____

_____

_____

_____

_____

_____

_____

                            Love,
                            Polly

Jovial Bob Stine gives expressions to use when writing thank-you notes. Would any of these expressions be helpful to you? Does he say some things you just don't believe? List the expressions you would use and the ones you would not use. Explain your choices.

Expressions you would use:

_____

_____

_____

_____

_____

_____

_____

_____

Expressions you would not use:

_____

_____

_____

_____

_____

_____

_____

_____

Share your lists with a group. Did you agree?

At different times in the story, characters felt various emotions. Look back through the story for examples of the following emotions. Write who felt the emotion and why.

enjoyment: _____

_____

_____

annoyance: _____

_____

_____

boredom: _____

_____

_____

delight: _____

_____

_____

frustration: _____

_____

_____

regret: _____

_____

_____

Use information from the story and your own ideas to complete the following.

William knew it was a real radio program going on inside his head, because _____

_____

_____

_____

_____

Having a real radio program going on inside his head worried William at first, because _____

_____

_____

_____

_____

When William realized that he had a built-in radio, he thought it was wonderful, because ____

_____

_____

_____

_____

William decided not to show off about his radio in the schoolyard, because _____

_____

_____

_____

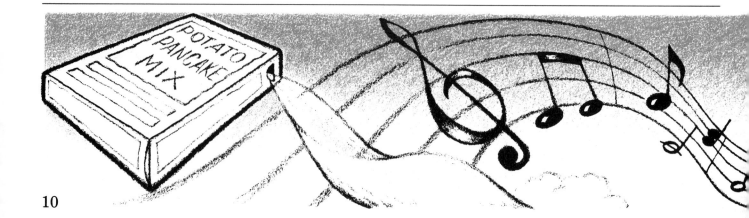

The kids at school liked to play tricks on Mr. Wendel, because _____

_____

_____

_____

Melvyn tried for as long as possible to let Mr. Wendel think he had the radio, because _____

_____

_____

_____

_____

Melvyn said "I'll never trust anyone in authority again," because _____

_____

_____

_____

_____

The children would "lay off out of sympathy" with other teachers, but not with Mr. Wendel,

because _____

_____

_____

_____

◆◆◆◆◆◆◆ "I WANT A LAWYER" ◆◆◆◆◆◆◆

When Mr. Wendel accuses Melvyn of having the radio, Melvyn seems to enjoy the moment. On page 27 both characters use the kind of language you might hear in a courtroom. Imagine you are Melvyn. Write "Melvyn's Guide to Legal Language" explaining the following terms so that other students may use them.

constitutional rights: _____

_____

_____

trial by a jury of my peers: _____

_____

_____

illegal search: _____

_____

_____

defence: _____

_____

_____

search warrant: _____

_____

_____

Mr. Wendel threatened Melvyn with Devil's Island. What do you think he meant? Where can you find out about Devil's Island? You might like to find out about Devil's Island with a classmate.

CONTRAST

In "Sleeping Ugly," Plain Jane and Princess Miserella are very different. One is very, very good, while the other is very, very bad. You could say they are opposites. This difference is called a contrast. How many contrasts can you find between these two characters?

Princess Miserella	Plain Jane

Appearance

_____   _____

_____   _____

_____   _____

_____   _____

Behaviour

_____   _____

_____   _____

_____   _____

_____   _____

_____   _____

_____   _____

Personality

_____   _____

_____   _____

_____   _____

_____   _____

Why do you think the author contrasted Princess Miserella and Plain Jane? How could you use contrast in one of your stories?

Imagine Plain Jane and the prince are having a dinner party. At the party they use the sleeping princess as a coatrack. Write a conversation you might hear between two guests about this unusual coatrack.

_____

_____

_____

_____

_____

_____

_____

_____

_____

Imagine that Plain Jane and the prince had two more dinner parties. At each party they used the sleeping princess in an unusual way. For each party decide how the sleeping princess was used and write a conversation between two guests about the sleeping princess in her new role.

Party #1

_____

_____

_____

_____

_____

_____

_____

_____

Party #2

_____

_____

_____

_____

_____

_____

_____

_____

_____

_____

What do you think a conversation piece is? You probably have a conversation piece in your own home. What is it? Write a conversation that might take place because of this piece.

_____

_____

_____

_____

_____

_____

_____

_____

_____

"Sleeping Ugly" is a fairy tale with a difference. It is a humorous version of another fairy tale which you are probably familiar with—"Sleeping Beauty." "Sleeping Ugly" has many of the same features as "Sleeping Beauty" and other fairy tales (a hero or heroine, a problem, a fairy godmother, a prince) but also many differences. Think back to the last time you heard or read "Sleeping Beauty." Now write down the similarities and differences between "Sleeping Ugly" and "Sleeping Beauty."

Similarities: _____

_____

_____

_____

_____

_____

_____

_____

Differences: _____

_____

_____

_____

_____

_____

_____

_____

_____

Share your ideas with a partner or two. Compare your ideas.

PORTRAIT OF EVIL

In the "Rise and Fall of Ben Gizzard," the author paints a picture of Ben as a "shrewd trader and a mean man." List examples from the story which add to this picture of Ben.

_____

_____

_____

_____

_____

_____

_____

_____

_____

_____

_____

_____

_____

_____

_____

_____

_____

_____

_____

_____

 # EXPLAIN YOURSELF!

In this story, the author, Richard Kennedy, uses interesting language to explain what he means. What do these sentences mean to you?

Ben had no use for Indian witchcraft or anything else he couldn't lay his hands on. (page 44)

_____

_____

_____

A fellow could get along just fine in the world if he kept watching things out of the corners of his eyes. (page 44)

_____

_____

_____

He could stand in one spot and look right around the corner of something good, and right behind it, and see the bad part of it. (page 44)

_____

_____

_____

The outcroppings of silver on the sides of the gulch shone like fillings in a dark mouth, and the mines went in like cavities. (page 44)

_____

_____

_____

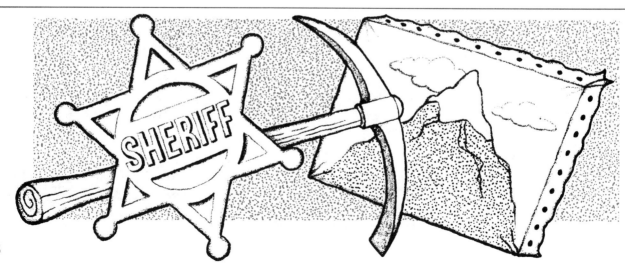

18

The day would not come to Depression Gulch when he would die for his wickedness. (page 46)

_____

_____

_____

"I ain't wearing silk shorts because I'm stupid." (page 47)

_____

_____

_____

He slid around town like a salamander. (page 48)

_____

_____

_____

Terror drove through Ben like a spike. (page 52)

_____

_____

_____

"I think you tried to burn me out of here." (page 55)

_____

_____

_____

Ben . . . like a snake, had a way of getting up close and confidential before he struck. (page 56)

_____

_____

_____

"I just want to show you my heart's in the right place." (page 56)

_____

_____

_____

Ben Gizzard started to take more chances with his life when he found out that he could not die except under very special circumstances. Is your behaviour based on the fact that if you misbehave, you have to face the consequences? Would you behave differently if there were no consequences?

If there were no punishment in school, what difference would it make?

_____

_____

_____

_____

Would it be a good thing? Why?

_____

_____

_____

_____

If no one ever watched you while you ate, what difference would it make?

_____

_____

_____

_____

Would it be a good thing? Why?

_____

_____

_____

_____

If you knew you could not injure any part of your body, what difference would it make?

_____

_____

_____

_____

Would it be a good thing? Why?

_____

_____

_____

_____

Give more ideas about how you would behave differently if there were no consequences.

_____

_____

_____

_____

_____

Share your ideas in a small group. Do you think consequences are good or bad? Why?

 # SAILORS' GLOSSARY

In Robin's account of his journey, he uses many words and phrases special to sailors. Here are some of them:

squall	shroud	mainsail	jib	knots	boom
jury rig	mast	trade winds	topside	forestay	athwart
backstay	foresail	sea legs	logbook	reefed jib	tack
doldrums	halyard	headstay	hull	marina	
lifeline harness		shipping lanes		taffrail log spinner	

A "glossary" is a type of dictionary that is often found at the end of a book. It lists and defines those words that the reader may be seeing for the first time. Look back through the story for the words and phrases listed above. List them in alphabetical order and write a definition for each using the information in the story and your own knowledge. To define any you do not know, you might do some research. (Do you know a sailor who could help you?)

_____

_____

_____

_____

_____

_____

_____

_____

_____

_____

_____

_____

_____

_____

_____

_____

In his entry for July 27, 1965, Robin recalls a mixture of experiences and feelings—some good and some bad. Imagine you are Robin keeping a log of your experiences at sea. Look back through the story. What incidents might you list under the following headings in your log?

Robin's Log

Good Experiences:

_____

_____

_____

_____

_____

_____

_____

_____

_____

Bad Experiences:

_____

_____

_____

_____

_____

_____

_____

_____

_____

Imagine you are going to make the same journey next year. Would you do anything differently? Would you take along anything else? Explain what changes you might make.

_____

_____

_____

_____

_____

_____

_____

_____

_____

_____

_____

_____

_____

_____

_____

_____

**Discuss your lists and your journey
plans with a classmate. Why do you think
people undertake adventures like this one?
Do you know of similar adventures?**

◆◆◆◆◆◆◆◆◆◆ IN ORDER TO . . . ◆◆◆◆◆◆◆◆◆

Look back through "The Wendigo" to complete the following sentences.

When the wealthy man got to the trading post, he tried to find a guide in order to _____

_____

DéFago took the job in order to _____

_____

During the storm, the hunter opened the tent flap in order to _____

_____

When DéFago began to run from the tent, the hunter wrestled him to the ground in order to

_____

_____

The hunter wanted to leave the place where the footprints ended in order to _____

_____

When the hunter left the camp as fast as he could, he left some food in order to _____

_____

IT'S JUST A CRAZY STORY, BUT . . .

What makes a story scary or spooky? Why do so many of them take place at night in a lonely place? Why do they often take place during storms? Explain how each of the following elements helps to make "The Wendigo" a spooky story.

Setting (time and place)

_____

_____

_____

_____

Characters

_____

_____

_____

_____

Mood (feeling)

_____

_____

_____

_____

Plot

_____

_____

_____

_____

Think of another spooky story you have heard or read. Describe the characters, setting, and any other elements that added to its spookiness. You might want to get together in a group to plan a spooky story.

Think back to all the scary stories you have heard or read. Which ones stand out in your mind? Why? Complete the following.

The scariest story I have ever read is _____

_____

The scariest story I have ever heard is _____

_____

The scariest movie I have ever seen is _____

_____

The scariest character I have ever seen or read about is _____

_____

Plan a scary story you might write in the future. Jot down some ideas about:

Setting (time and place)

_____

_____

_____

Characters

_____

_____

_____

Plot

_____

_____

_____

Now you can write your own story and share it with your friends.

28

The author of *Children of the Wolf* uses colourful language to paint word pictures in your mind as you read the story. Go back through this excerpt and find the words and phrases Jane Yolen uses to paint pictures of the following.

The wolf-children didn't like being washed. (page 83)

_____

_____

Mrs. Welles was quite soaked. (page 83)

_____

_____

The wolf-children looked different from other children. (pages 82-85)

_____

_____

Rama, Veda, and Indira played like wolves. (page 85)

_____

_____

The wolf-children felt more comfortable with the puppies than with humans. (page 87)

_____

_____

List some more descriptive words and phrases that are used in the story. Add some of your own words and phrases to the list.

_____   _____

_____   _____

_____   _____

_____   _____

Mr. Welles tells the children at the orphanage not to frighten the wolf-children, but to treat them kindly. Unlike the other children, the narrator of the story seems to have considered the wolf-children's feelings already, judging by his kindness to them. How does Mohandas show this . . .

when the other children talk about the bath?

_____

_____

_____

when Indira says the calluses are "horrible"?

_____

_____

_____

when the other children scorn "running on all fours"?

_____

_____

_____

when the wolf-girl bays at the moon?

_____

_____

_____

 # SOON THEY WILL REWARD US . . .

Mr. Welles also says "Soon they will reward us with tales of the jungle and stories of wonders such as mankind rarely beholds." Imagine you are one of the wolf-children. You begin to trust Mohandas and want to tell him about your life with the wolves. Plan the tale you would tell to Mohandas by writing your ideas under the following headings.

Setting (time, place): _____

_____

_____

_____

_____

_____

Main characters: _____

_____

_____

_____

_____

_____

_____

Events of the day we were captured: _____

_____

_____

_____

_____

_____

_____

Now you can write your tale!

 I THINK I KNOW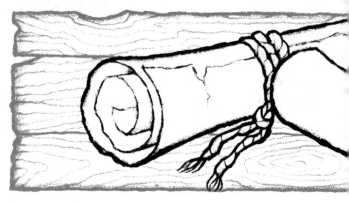

As this story is set in Norman England 800 years ago, some of the language may be unfamiliar to you. Find the following words and phrases in the selection. Read the part that comes just before and after. Write down what you think each word might mean. Don't use a dictionary yet.

cottars (page 93): _____

_____

_____

_____

scythes (page 93): _____

_____

_____

_____

turf balk (page 93): _____

_____

_____

_____

flitch (page 93): _____

_____

_____

_____

villeins (page 93): _____

_____

_____

_____

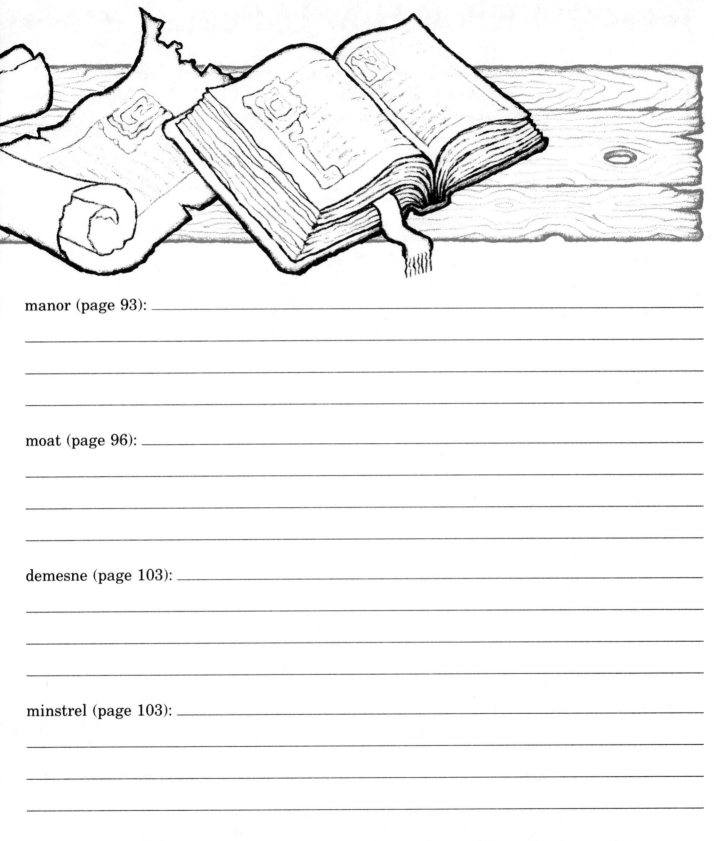

manor (page 93): _____

_____

_____

_____

moat (page 96): _____

_____

_____

_____

demesne (page 103): _____

_____

_____

_____

minstrel (page 103): _____

_____

_____

_____

Get together with a group of classmates to discuss your definitions. Use your dictionaries and other reference materials. Compare your definitions and add to them. Discuss the words *you* might use instead. Why do words change? Can you think of other words that have changed over time?

How do you think Clac and his friends felt when they first saw the green children? How do you think the green children felt when they saw Clac and his friends? Look back through the story. Who might be feeling the following emotions? When?

nervousness: _____

_____

_____

curiosity: _____

_____

_____

fear: _____

_____

_____

excitement: _____

_____

_____

puzzlement: _____

_____

_____

loneliness: _____

_____

_____

Think of another emotion that might be felt in the story. Who might be feeling it? When?

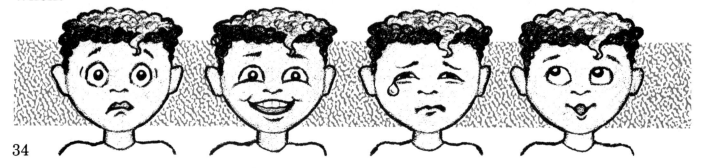

34

When the green girl learned to speak English, she told Sir Richard and the others at the manor her story. "But that was only the beginning. Many were the questions asked of her that night; many were the answers given." Imagine you were at Sir Richard's manor that night. Write down some questions you would have liked to ask the green girl. After each question, write her answer.

Question #1: _____

_____

_____

_____

Question #2: _____

_____

_____

_____

Question #3: _____

_____

_____

_____

_____

_____

_____

_____

_____

_____

_____

_____

Work with a partner. One of you can role-play the green child and the other asks the questions. Switch parts.

Often an author leaves the reader to figure out exactly what the characters are thinking, and why they are behaving as they are. (You have to read between the lines to do this.) Read between the following lines and write down what you think the author is saying.

In the ruler-straight rows of desks and chairs, the seventh graders fidgeted. (page 112)

_____

_____

_____

Mr. Radagast finally realized that a student had been asking him questions. The novelty of the situation surprised him . . . (page 114)

_____

_____

_____

. . . his students were all staring at him as though he'd sprouted orange warts and an extra pair of ears. (page 114)

_____

_____

_____

Groans filled the classroom, twenty-eight groans from twenty-eight throats. (page 115)

_____

_____

_____

Luckily for Damon, he had a lot of classes like this one where he could work without fear of distraction. (page 115)

_____

_____

_____

"Why, yes!" Mr. Radagast said eagerly. He couldn't believe his good fortune. (page 115)

_____

_____

_____

Sixty eyes stared at the front of the room. Thirty minds all thought the same thought. (page 118)

_____

_____

_____

His perfect teeth trembled. His eyes were glazed with anticipation, dreams of future glory. (page 118)

_____

_____

_____

Thirty mouths fell open. Thirty bodies thumped back against their chairs. (page 118)

_____

_____

_____

Get together with a group of classmates to compare your answers.

DULL OR NOT?

Mr. Radagast's science lessons always seemed dull to his students. Use information from the story and your own ideas to explain why you think his lessons were boring.

_____

_____

_____

_____

_____

_____

Think about things you have learned in school. What has made learning interesting for you?

_____

_____

_____

_____

_____

_____

What has made learning dull and boring?

_____

_____

_____

When you have finished you might like to share your ideas with some classmates. Perhaps you could write a book sharing your ideas on how to make learning interesting. Write a short description of what could be in each chapter.

Title: _____

Chapter 1: _____

_____

_____

_____

Chapter 2: _____

_____

_____

_____

_____

_____

_____

_____

_____

_____

_____

_____

**Find the following words and
phrases in the story and read the part
that comes just before and just after.
Then explain what you think each means.**

The privileged six (page 112)

_____

_____

conceptions of space and time (page 113)

_____

_____

theoretically correct (page 114)

_____

_____

the baleful glare of his classmates (page 114)

_____

_____

visual aid (page 114)

_____

_____

sense of social prerogative (page 114)

_____

_____

EVERLASTING

The Tuck family had mixed feelings about living forever. They mention some of their reasons. What other reasons might they have? Use information from the story and your own ideas to list the advantages and disadvantages of living forever.

Advantages: _____

_____

_____

_____

_____

_____

_____

_____

_____

Disadvantages: _____

_____

_____

_____

_____

_____

_____

_____

If you could, would you choose to drink from the magic stream, or not? Why? Share your decision and reasons with some classmates.

Look back through the excerpt from *Tuck Everlasting* to help you respond to the following.

Mae said, "The cat didn't drink. That's important." Why was it important?

_____

_____

_____

"The horse was out grazing by some trees and they shot him . . . But the thing is, they didn't kill him." Why didn't the horse die?

_____

_____

_____

"But it was the passage of time that worried them most." Why?

_____

_____

_____

Jesse says, "I'm glad *I* never got married." Why does he say that?

_____

_____

_____

42

"Well, you can't hardly blame them." Whom is Mae referring to? Why couldn't she blame them?

_____

_____

_____

Mae says, "We was like gypsies." The Tuck family had to keep moving. Why?

_____

_____

_____

"And the T he'd carved was as fresh as if it'd just been put there." Why?

_____

_____

_____

"We're still talking it over," Jesse added. Why would the family still be talking it over?

_____

_____

_____

"We don't know how it works, or even why," says Miles. What is it that is working? Can you offer any explanations for "it" working the way it does?

_____

_____

_____

"Some plan that didn't work out too good. And so everything was changed." What type of plan could this have been?

_____

_____

_____

MY SPEECH — YOUR SPEECH

The Tuck family speaks in dialect. A dialect is a difference in words or pronunciation, often associated with where you live or where you learned to speak English. For example, Mae says, "But come to find out, it didn't hurt him a bit." What do you think Mae is saying? How would you say the same thing? Find and write down other examples of the dialect the Tuck family uses. After each one, write what you would say.

_____

_____

_____

_____

_____

_____

_____

_____

_____

_____

_____

_____

_____

_____

_____

_____

_____

When you have finished, get together in a small group and talk about your responses. Do you all share the same dialect? What differences are there? Why? Can you find examples of other dialects in your neighbourhood?

Look back through the story to find examples to support the following statements:

Unusual things often happened at the Armitage house on Mondays.

For instance, _____

_____

_____

Because it is Tuesday, Mr. and Mrs. Armitrage try to act as if nothing unusual has happened.

For instance, _____

_____

_____

The unicorn seems to understand English.

For instance, _____

_____

_____

The unicorn seemed quite pleased about being shod.

For instance, _____

_____

_____

The little old man in a red cloak seemed to have magical powers.

For instance, _____

_____

_____

Getting back home presented some difficulties for the children.

For instance, _____

_____

_____

AND IT'S A BEAUTY...

The author of "Yes, But Today is Tuesday" uses colourful words and phrases to paint word pictures in your mind. Look back through the story to find the descriptive language Joan Aiken uses to paint these pictures.

Harriet noticed that the unicorn's horn and feet had a green glow. (page 140)

_____

_____

A unicorn tear fell on Harriet's hand. (page 141)

_____

_____

A storm started. (page 145)

_____

_____

Using descriptive language, paint a word picture of the scene Mr. Armitage saw when he first noticed the one hundred unicorns on his lawn.

_____

_____

_____

_____

_____

_____

_____

 # SHE KNEW THAT!

When the little old man threatened to cast a spell on the unicorn, Harriet said, "We've had it shod. You haven't any power over it anymore." What information do *you* know about unicorns and these other mythical creatures?

Unicorns: _____

_____

_____

Werewolves: _____

_____

_____

Sasquatch or Bigfoot: _____

_____

_____

What other mythical creatures have you heard of? Write down anything you know about each one.

_____

_____

_____

_____

_____

_____

_____

_____

_____

_____

Get together with a classmate or two to share your information.

Imagine that you are going to make a movie called "The Foundling." Your movie should be shot around a series of important scenes from the story. The first scene might show Orwen, Orddu and Orgoch finding the baby in the Marshes of Morva. Plan all the important scenes that will make up your movie and describe what happens in each one.

Scene 1: _____

_____

_____

_____

_____

_____

_____

_____

_____

_____

_____

_____

_____

_____

_____

_____

_____

_____

_____

_____

_____

DECISIONS

Imagine you are Dallben. Explain the reasons for some of the decisions you have made in your life.

When the hags offered me my choice of gifts, I almost took the sword because _____

_____

_____

But I didn't, because _____

_____

_____

I almost took the golden harp because _____

_____

_____

But I didn't, because _____

_____

_____

I took the book of wisdom because _____

_____

_____

With the last few pages unread, I almost destroyed the book because _____

_____

_____

But I didn't, because _____

_____

_____

DEAR DIARY...

Imagine you are Helen; you are going to try to keep a diary this year. Think back over your first day in Grade Six. What good things happened? What bad things?

Write your diary entry.

Sometimes you have to read between the lines of the story to figure out why a character is behaving in a certain way. Look back through the story and read between the lines to find the reason for each character's behaviour.

Mother wanted to pat down Helen's clothing before she went to school.

_____

_____

One little girl told her friend, "That's 'Bad Helen,' " as Helen passed by.

_____

_____

Helen put on her best I-don't-care smile when she didn't get Mr. Marshall for her teacher after all.

_____

_____

Playing baseball at recess, Helen forgot about school, but going back in, her stomach started to hurt.

_____

_____

When Mrs. Lobb asked Helen, "How do you spell 'mean'?" Jack answered.

_____

_____

Helen ran all the way back to school to get her reading book.

_____

_____

_____

_____

_____

Think back to your first day of school this year. Write a page of "First Day Hints" for someone entering your grade next September. Will you give hints about people? rules? procedures? supplies? lunchtime?

_____

_____

_____

_____

_____

_____

_____

_____

_____

_____

_____

_____

_____

_____

_____

_____

_____

_____

_____

_____

_____

Perhaps you could share your ideas with two or three classmates and then create a booklet of first day hints.

This is not an easy summer for Jeremy and Sarah. Some things are happening that make them feel worried. Other things make them feel angry. Here is a list of how they might be feeling: worried, angry, understanding, afraid, upset, calm. For each of these "feeling words" explain why Jeremy or Sarah might be having those feelings.

_____

_____

_____

_____

_____

_____

_____

_____

_____

_____

_____

_____

_____

_____

_____

_____

_____

_____

_____

_____

_____

Have you ever had these same feelings? When? Why? Choose two or three feelings and explain what caused you to feel that way.

◆◆◆◆◆◆◆◆ ONE MORE TIME ◆◆◆◆◆◆◆◆

Here are some sentences and phrases from the story. Find each one and read the part that comes just before and just after. Write what you think each italicized phrase means.

Lost in his thoughts, he had not known she was there until she spoke. (page 182)

_____

She held her tongue and went on waiting. (page 183)

_____

She has *enough to bear* without that. (page 184)

_____

Straightening her out on so many things at once made him feel better. (page 186)

_____

He *hardened his heart.* (page 186)

_____

Outraged at this *veiled threat,* he stopped feeling even faintly sorry for her. (page 186)

_____

. . . and yet he could *twist the truth* so cleverly . . . (page 187)

_____

. . . keeping his tone *matter of fact.* (page 187)

_____

Use experiences from your own life to respond to the following.

When do you become *lost in thought?*

_____

_____

_____

When have you had to *hold your tongue?*

_____

_____

_____

When have you had to *straighten somebody out?*

_____

_____

_____

Have you ever had to *harden your heart?*

_____

_____

_____

Have you ever given or received a *veiled threat?*

_____

_____

_____

When have you heard someone *twist the truth?*

_____

_____

_____

Discuss your answers in a group. How do your experiences differ? How are they the same?

HOLIDAY MEMORIES

In this selection the author recalls the sights, sounds, and smells at Woolworth's during the holidays. Classify the following memories under the appropriate heading.

squeaky wooden floors   long red and silver fuzzy streamers   hot dogs and fried eggs

Now look back through the selection to find more sense memories and classify them. Add some memories of holiday times from your own experience.

Sights	Sounds	Smells
_____	_____	_____
_____	_____	_____
_____	_____	_____
_____	_____	_____
_____	_____	_____
_____	_____	_____
_____	_____	_____
_____	_____	_____
_____	_____	_____
_____	_____	_____
_____	_____	_____
_____	_____	_____
_____	_____	_____
_____	_____	_____

Think of places where the sights, sounds, and smells create a special atmosphere. Choose a place; go there to observe and make notes, recording below the sights, sounds and smells.

Sights	Sounds	Smells
_____	_____	_____
_____	_____	_____
_____	_____	_____
_____	_____	_____
_____	_____	_____

Now use these words to write a descriptive paragraph about the place you chose.

_____

_____

_____

_____

_____

_____

_____

_____

_____

_____

_____

The story says that Santa Claus (Ozzie O'Driscoll) would tell the children "a whole lot of stuff they never heard before about the North Pole. Like how Mrs. Claus used to hit him over the head . . . how sick he'd be after making his rounds and eating all the stuff everybody left out for him." What other things might Ozzie have told the children that they might never have heard before.

_____

_____

_____

_____

_____

_____

_____

_____

_____

_____

_____

Santa Claus (Ozzie O'Driscoll) asked the kids to suggest easy names for his reindeer so he could remember them. What names would you suggest?

_____   _____

_____   _____

_____   _____

And what about the one with the bright nose?

60

Use information from *Grandma Didn't Wave Back,* and your own ideas to find evidence for the following.

Friday night had always been special for Grandma.

_____

_____

Debbie didn't like it now when her relatives came over.

_____

_____

Debbie felt she had a special relationship with Grandma.

_____

_____

Debbie's parents had to do something soon.

_____

_____

Debbie felt she had to go on her own to visit Grandma for the first time.

_____

_____

Grandma was getting Debbie ready for the time when they would not be together anymore.

_____

When Debbie went to visit Grandma, she took along some things she knew Grandma cherished. Why might Grandma have valued these things so highly? What memories might they hold? Use your imagination. Write down what you think each of these "cherished things" means to Grandma.

the flowered shawl

_____

_____

the clock

_____

_____

the china fruit basket

_____

_____

the few carved dishes

_____

_____

the beautiful seagull

_____

_____

the tsotzkes (you might need to do some research here)

_____

_____

USED-TO-BE'S

Debbie says, "You know, Mom, . . . when you start to grow up, there are lots more used-to-be's." You are growing up. What are some "used-to-be's" of your life?

POINTS OF VIEW

The day that Gilly's grandmother came to see her was certainly an eventful day. As Gilly says, the house had become a "looney bin." Gilly is in a foster home and Miss Ellis is her caseworker. Imagine that Gilly writes a short letter to her explaining what was going on.

_____

_____

_____

_____

_____

_____

_____

_____

_____

_____

_____

_____

_____

_____

_____

_____

Yours truly,
Gilly Hopkins

Try to look at the events of that visit from Gilly's grandmother's point of view. Might the grandmother see things differently? Write the letter from Gilly's grandmother to Miss Ellis.

_____

_____

_____

_____

_____

_____

_____

_____

_____

_____

_____

_____

_____

_____

_____

_____

_____

_____

_____

Yours truly,
Gilly's Grandmother

Some of the words and phrases used by the characters in the story may be unfamiliar to you. Read the following sentences, then write in your own words what the italicized words mean.

So with many rest stops for Trotter *to recapture her wind*, she and Gilly brought the rollaway cot. (page 206)

_____

_____

Trotter . . . maintained that there was some *moral obligation* to inform next of kin when one took to one's bed. (page 207)

_____

_____

You have my *solemn oath*. (page 207)

_____

_____

Gilly, if he looks *peaky*, we carry him next door . . . (page 207)

_____

_____

By then, both Trotter and William Ernest were both *down with the bug*. (page 207)

_____

_____

She was simply *too whipped* to pick up after herself. (page 208)

_____

_____

She had always been—existing from before time—*like a goddess in perpetual perfection.*
(pages 209-210)

_____

_____

Her voice was Southern but smooth, *like silk to Trotter's burlap.* (page 210)

_____

_____

Swaying in the doorway was a *huge barefoot apparition* in striped man's pajamas . . .
(page 213)

_____

_____

The visitor, for her part, was *teetering on the absolute brink* of the brown chair in what Gilly
took to be a state of total shock. (page 215)

_____

_____

She had no wish for the woman to *think poorly* of her. (page 215)

_____

_____

Get together with a friend to compare your responses.

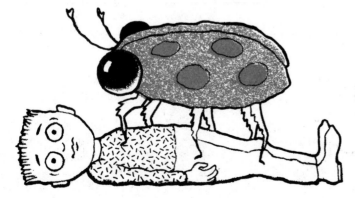

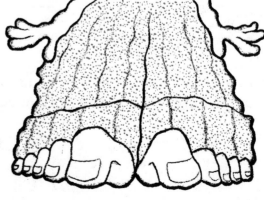

The selection "Lucy Maud Montgomery" is a "biography" because it tells the story of someone's life. What did you learn about Lucy Maud Montgomery from the selection? Make a list of words you would use to describe Lucy Maud Montgomery.

_____   _____   _____

_____   _____   _____

_____   _____   _____

Choose several words from your list and explain why you think each one fits.

Word: _____

Reasons: _____

_____

_____

Word: _____

Reasons: _____

_____

_____

Word: _____

Reasons: _____

_____

_____

Word: _____

Reasons: _____

_____

_____

Share your responses with a friend. What words would you use to write an _autobiography_ (a biography of yourself)?

A time line is an arrangement of events in the order that they took place. Excerpt the information from L.M. Montgomery's biography to complete the time line of major events in her life started below.

Age 21 months (1876): came to live with her grandparents, the MacNeills

Age 6

Age 9

Get together with a partner to compare your time lines.

WHAT I'D LIKE TO BE

Lucy Maud Montgomery was determined to be recognized as a writer. List a few of the things that Maud did to help make her dream come true.

_____

_____

_____

_____

Do you have a dream of what you would like to be when you are older? What would you like to be?

_____

_____

_____

_____

_____

_____

Write down some hints that could help you realize your dreams.

How to Get There

_____

_____

_____

_____

_____

_____

_____

_____

_____

_____

HIGHS AND LOWS

In this excerpt of the play, *Anne of Green Gables*, Anne's emotions range from extreme happiness to thorough misery. Look back through this excerpt to find examples of things Anne says and does to show these opposite emotions.

Extreme happiness:

words: _____

_____

_____

_____

_____

actions: _____

_____

_____

_____

_____

Thorough misery:

words: _____

_____

_____

_____

_____

actions: _____

_____

_____

_____

_____

Anne is a very imaginative child. To her the world is "rose-in-bloomy, you can think the things you want to be." What are some signs of Anne's imagination at work?

_____

_____

_____

_____

_____

_____

_____

_____

_____

_____

_____

_____

_____

_____

_____

_____

_____

_____

_____

Anne asks, "Which would you rather be if you had your wish? Divinely beautiful? or dazzlingly clever? or angelically good?" Before you make a choice, write down some ideas about . . .

being divinely beautiful

_____

_____

_____

_____

_____

being dazzlingly clever

_____

_____

_____

_____

_____

being angelically good

_____

_____

_____

_____

_____

Well, which would you choose to be—divinely beautiful, dazzingly clever, or angelically good? Why?

_____

_____

_____

_____

 # A CHANGE WILL DO YOU GOOD

Imagine that Anne does end up staying with Matthew and Marilla. How might Anne change their lives? Write your ideas in the space below. (Look back through the excerpt for hints.)

_____

_____

_____

_____

_____

_____

_____

_____

_____

_____

_____

_____

_____

_____

_____

_____

_____

_____

_____

Share your ideas with some classmates.

Imagine you are a reporter for the local newspaper and were standing beside the judges' stand when the commotion started. Write a news report explaining what happened. Remember, a reporter must answer the questions "Who?" "What?" "When?" "Where?" and "Why?" What will your eye-catching headline be?

WEATHER

Saskatoon Times

EARLY MORNING EDITION 25¢

_____

_____

_____

_____

_____

_____

_____

_____

_____

_____

_____

_____

_____

_____

_____

_____

_____

_____

_____

_____

_____

_____

Imagine you are the narrator in *Owls in the Family*. You are in charge of preparing your float for the pet parade. The parade is in two weeks. Look back through the story for information to help you write instructions for you and your friends to follow. Who will do what? How? When?

_____

_____

_____

_____

_____

_____

_____

_____

_____

_____

_____

_____

_____

_____

_____

_____

_____

_____

_____

_____

_____

_____

_____

_____

_____

_____

_____

_____

_____

You still think you should have won first prize in the pet parade. Write a short note to the judges explaining why you think you should have won and asking them to reconsider their decision.

_____

_____

_____

_____

_____

_____

_____

_____

_____

 # THE EXPERIMENT

Katherine McKeever, the author of *Granny's Gang*, performs many experiments using Pops and young owls. Use information from the story to write a report on the experiment with Pops and Mildred.

Purpose: _____

_____

_____

_____

Method: _____

_____

_____

_____

_____

_____

Observations: _____

_____

_____

_____

_____

_____

_____

Conclusions: _____

_____

_____

_____

Both the owls and the people in this story show different feelings at different times. The owlets "hreep" when they're anxious, but feelings can be shown in other ways. Look back through the story to find who felt the following feelings and why. How were these feelings shown? (There may be more than one example of each feeling.)

confusion: _____

_____

_____

excitement: _____

_____

_____

helplessness: _____

_____

_____

worry: _____

_____

_____

nervousness: _____

_____

_____

delight: _____

_____

_____

OWL GLOSSARY

◆◆◆◆◆◆◆

◆◆◆◆◆◆◆

Look back through *Granny's Gang* to find the following words. Create an owl glossary by writing a definition or explanation for each one. Add any other information you know.

species (page 244): _____

_____

ruff (page 244): _____

_____

talons (page 245): _____

_____

owlet (page 245): _____

_____

juvenile (page 245): _____

_____

instinct (page 245): _____

_____

platform nest (page 246): _____

_____

Discuss your responses with some classmates.

◆◆◆ SCAPULARS AND SECONDARIES ◆◆◆

This is an exercise in observation. Complete this page without using any reference books. (You may do that later.) Do you know the names of the birds you see in your environment? Have you ever seen a robin? A white-breasted nuthatch? A bluejay? List the names of birds you've seen.

_____ _____ _____

_____ _____ _____

_____ _____ _____

How good are your observation skills? Choose one of the birds from your list and, using some of the terms in "Looking at Birds," describe the appearance of this bird. What colour are its scapulars? Does it have wing bars? (You may want to draw and label the bird.)

Now check a reference book. How accurate is your observation of the bird's appearance? You may want to change or add to your description.

 # SHARK SHEET

The article on sharks contains different types of information. Look back through the article to find information and classify it under the following headings. Then add any further information you know about sharks.

History: _____

_____

_____

_____

Habitat (where they live): _____

_____

_____

_____

Physical Characteristics: _____

_____

_____

_____

Behaviour: _____

_____

_____

_____

Other information: _____

_____

_____

_____

Get together with a partner to share your Shark Sheet.

THE PERFECT CYCLE

The article states that: "Life in the sea, as on land, is a complete and perfect cycle." Look back through "Sharks" to understand the food cycle of the sea. Draw and label this "perfect cycle" in the space below.

Read Chief Seattle's words at the end of the article on sharks. What do you think he means by " . . . loneliness of spirit"? Do you think whatever happens to the beasts soon happens to humankind? How are all things connected? Write your thoughts.

_____

_____

_____

_____

_____

_____

_____

_____

_____

_____

_____

_____

_____

_____

_____

_____

_____

_____

_____

_____

Sometimes you have to read between the lines to understand why the characters say or do certain things. Read between the lines and write what you think about the following:

Why does the Sevillano call the Manta Diablo Ramón's friend when he says, "Your friend shows off"? (page 260)

_____

_____

Why does the Sevillano say "I have killed nine mantas"? (page 260)

_____

_____

"I hesitated to answer him, confused as I was by what I had just heard and by his question." (page 263) Why was Ramón confused?

_____

_____

The Manta Diablo "swam slowly, so that no water came aboard, as if he did not wish to disturb us in any way." (page 266) Why?

_____

_____

The Sevillano acted "like a magician getting ready for an act." (page 267) Why?

_____

_____

The Manta Diablo "raised his fins over his back, as if to brush the Sevillano away." (page 269) What does this mean to you?

_____

_____

Scott O'Dell paints word pictures in your mind with his use of descriptive language. Decide whether the descriptions below create a sight or sound scene in your mind. Write "sight" or "sound" beside each.

_____   "I heard the chattering of its green teeth . . ."

_____   " . . . the flash of his white undersides and his long tail
                                    whipping about."

Find other sentences or parts of sentences in the story that paint vivid pictures.

Sights

_____

_____

_____

_____

_____

_____

Sounds

_____

_____

_____

_____

_____

_____

Think of an occasion when you have been on or near the sea or another body of water. Write some words or phrases to describe the sights and sounds you experienced.

_____   _____

_____   _____

_____   _____

Now write a description of your experience.

_____

_____

_____

_____

_____

_____

_____

_____

_____

_____

_____

_____

_____

_____

_____

_____

As you read this excerpt from *The Black Pearl,* you learn a great deal about Gaspar Ruiz, the Sevillano. Is he all good? all bad? Look back through the story to get clues about the kind of person he is. Write a list of words that describe the character of the Sevillano.

_____   _____   _____

_____   _____   _____

_____   _____   _____

Choose several of the words you have used to describe the character of the Sevillano. Use information from the story to explain why you think each word is suitable.

Word: _____

Reasons: _____

_____

_____

Word: _____

Reasons: _____

_____

_____

Word: _____

Reasons: _____

_____

_____

Word: _____

Reasons: _____

_____

_____

Share your ideas with a partner. Did you see the same things in the character?

I HAVE MY REASONS

At the end of *Rabbit Island*, Big Grey feels he has to return to his "home." Little Brown feels he has to keep going to find his home. They both have their reasons. Write what you think each of them is thinking when they make their decisions.

Big Grey: _____

_____

_____

_____

_____

_____

_____

Little Brown: _____

_____

_____

_____

_____

_____

Does this story raise any questions in your mind? What does it make you think about? Write down any thoughts you have after reading the story.

_____

_____

_____

_____

Get together with a classmate or two to compare your thoughts or questions.

◆◆◆ CONVEYOR BELTS AND CLOVER ◆◆◆

When Little Brown arrived at the rabbit factory, Big Grey said, "If there's anything you want to know, you can just ask me. I've been living here a long time—a long, long time." He knew about the factory, but he had forgotten many things that Little Brown knew about the outside world. Think about the differences between the factory rabbits and the wild rabbits. Would the wild rabbit ever hear a conveyor belt? Would a factory rabbit ever taste clover? Use information from the story, and your own ideas to compare the sensory experiences of the two kinds of rabbits.

Sights

Wild Rabbits   Factory Rabbits

_____   _____

_____   _____

_____   _____

_____   _____

_____   _____

Sounds

Wild Rabbits   Factory Rabbits

_____   _____

_____   _____

_____   _____

_____   _____

_____   _____

Tastes

Wild Rabbits

_____

_____

_____

_____

_____

Factory Rabbits

_____

_____

_____

_____

_____

Smells

Wild Rabbits

_____

_____

_____

_____

_____

Factory Rabbits

_____

_____

_____

_____

_____

Touches

Wild Rabbits

_____

_____

_____

_____

_____

Factory Rabbits

_____

_____

_____

_____

_____

◆◆◆◆ AS I FINISH THIS BOOK... ◆◆◆◆

Now that you have come to the end of *Wherever You Are*, you have talked and written about a lot of stories and poems. The next few pages will give you a chance to think about the literature you have read, and to write some of your thoughts and memories. When you are finished, it might be interesting to compare your thoughts with some of your classmates.

I remember laughing: _____

_____

_____

_____

I remember feeling sad: _____

_____

_____

_____

I remember being curious: _____

_____

_____

_____

I remember scary moments: _____

_____

_____

Some characters stand out in my mind.

_____

_____

_____

_____

_____

_____

_____

_____

_____

_____

_____

_____

_____

_____

_____

_____

_____

Some of the stories and poems I read gave me ideas for my own writing. Let me tell you about some of the them: _____

_____

_____

_____

_____

_____

_____

_____

_____

If I were going to read a story to someone, I would choose one of these three:

1. _____

Reason: _____

_____

_____

2. _____

Reason: _____

_____

_____

3. _____

Reason: _____

_____

_____

I learned some things from the stories and poems in *Wherever You Are.*

I learned about differences between authors: _____

_____

_____

_____

_____

I learned about different styles of illustration: _____

_____

_____

_____

_____

I learned that my classmates and I didn't always agree when we talked about the literature: _

_____

_____

_____

_____

I learned some things about myself: _____

_____

_____

_____

_____

_____

_____

Some of the selections left questions in my mind. Here are some things I would like to find out more about.

Inquiry #1

What I want to find out: _____

_____

_____

How I might find out: _____

_____

_____

Inquiry #2

What I want to find out: _____

_____

_____

How I might find out: _____

_____

_____

Inquiry #3

What I want to find out: _____

_____

_____

How I might find out: _____

_____